Everyday Leadership
The Christian's Guide to Managing Yourself and Others

Eddie Snipes

A book by:
Exchanged Life Discipleship

Published by GES Book Publishing
Carrollton, GA

Copyright © 2013 by Eddie Snipes, Exchanged Life
Discipleship, and GES Book Publishing

http://www.exchangedlife.com

ISBN-13:9780615944869

Contact the author by visiting
http://www.exchangedlife.com or
http://www.eddiesnipes.com

Picture Credits
Front cover photo(s)purchased at: dreamstime.com

Table of Contents

Introduction

Not everyone has the natural ability to lead others, but everyone should be a leader in one sense. Your life is an influence on someone. Some have the idea that leadership is to be at the head of a mob. Some put their finger in the air, see where the wind is blowing, and then rush to take the lead. That type of person may have a Type-A personality, but they are not a leader. Type-A personalities are often effective leaders, but even non-leaders can have strong personalities.

A Type-A personality is the alpha dog. It's the person who is driven to be at the head of the pack. This type of personality may come in varying packages, such as the person who is first to step up to lead a group, game, or meeting. It could also be the person who is driven to be seen or to be the one in charge of everything. The most effective leadership type is the one who takes the lead rather than demanding to have their way.

A true leader does not make decisions based on where the group is going, but rather is the person who influences the direction of the group. Even the introvert can show true leadership.

When my children were very young, they got into mischief with a friend. Afterward I asked, "Why did you do this? You knew better."

One of my children said, "Joe-Bob was doing it, so we did it too."

Wrong answer. This is when I sat them down and explained how to be a leader, even when a stronger personality is taking charge. "A true leader is the person who does what is right – regardless of what others are doing. You don't have to be leading the group to be a leader. Sometimes a leader is the one who simply says, 'I don't think this is right.'"

I've seen many leaders interfere with group-think by merely asking the question, "Is this the best course of action?"

Group-think is when an entire group acts as one based on the direction and decision making of the rest of the group. They may not feel right about the action of the group, but they go along with it because everyone else is doing it. Yet one person can affect group-think and become the leader who snaps others out of this hypnotic way of thinking.

Many years back I was asked to serve on a leadership team in a church. The leadership team acted as an elder board and served as a check and balance in the church's leadership. Any expense over a certain amount needed to be approved by the leadership team. On one of my first meetings, one of the executive pastors presented a computer purchase for approval. He explained that he had weighed all the options and decided purchasing from a specific company was the best course of action. When he gave the price, I was surprised. It was ten times the price of most major brands of computers, didn't come with a service contract, and we would have to buy a monitor.

I watched six other men vote yes and no one questioned the excessive price. Then it came to my vote and I said, "Let's talk about this." When I began to explain how the price seemed a bit unreasonable, then each one of the men started discussing the issue. Every one of these men stated they didn't feel right about this, yet not one was willing to question it until someone took the lead.

This is human nature. No one wants to be the odd man out, but once you step up, you will often discover you aren't alone. Even the introvert has the power to influence others by example, asking a question that forces people to re-evaluate, sharing their reservations, or even by offering confirmation of a course of action.

One day a college professor illustrated the power of group think by conducting a class experiment. The task was to pick out the longest of three lines drawn on a piece of paper, but the test was set up for failure. In each class, he prepped all but two or three students to intentionally pick the shorter of the three lines. The few students who were in the dark watched the entire class declare that one of the shorter lines were the longest. Though the longest line was clearly the right answer, the majority of students went with the class consensus. Afterward, most explained how they knew they were picking the wrong line, but felt they would look dumb for being the only one who saw it differently. Some even thought they were the one wrong since it wasn't possible that everyone else could be wrong.

As a leader, we must learn to discern when something is worth fighting for and when something is not worthy of robbing our peace, but we also must learn to trust in our discernment.

In this book, we will look at practical ways to exercise leadership, influence others in positive ways, and how to resolve conflicts in a positive manner. The first order of business is to establish your own heart in confidence, for until you are secure with who you are, you are not capable of leading others – at least not in a healthy and effective way.

Let me reiterate an important truth. Leadership does not mean you have to be in charge. A leader is someone who influences others in positive ways. A true leader is not the person looking for credit or self-glorification. A true leader is someone who seeks to influence, encourage, and establish others as they reach for a common goal.

Some people view leadership as forcing others to conform to their ideals or ambitions. A true leader does not force others from behind, drag others against their will, use people for selfish ambition, or bully others into submission. Managing by intimidation or degrading others is not leadership.

A husband can intimidate his wife into submission, but this makes it impossible for her to stand with him. A boss can bully his employees, but all he will get is minimum effort and resistance. Most of that resistance will be passive-aggressive.

Those under this type of leadership may give a superficial form of submission, but unless it is founded upon mutual respect, human nature on both sides will undermine the goal. A parent can crush their children with rules, punishment, and intimidation, but the end result will be a child who rebels against the family. It may be open rebellion in the home, or become a rejection of values when they leave home. An employee may have a form of submission, but once something challenges their loyalty, they will abandon the goal – unless they have adopted the same values as that of the leadership.

Unless leadership builds up others, builds trust, or causes others to believe in the direction the leader is going, the goal will never be effectively communicated or implemented. Until someone in a subordinate position believes in our leadership, any effort to be an influence will be limited in its effectiveness.

True leadership teaches others to value what you value and to desire what you desire. When someone buys into your vision, you won't need strong handed tactics to maintain control. Using intimidation only shows we lack confidence in ourselves, others, our vision, or all the above. A confident leader is not intimidated; therefore, he or she does not need to intimidate others.

These leadership skills apply to business, church, marriage, and parenting. The concept of leading doesn't change. The environment may change and the personalities you deal with may affect how you apply your leadership skills, but these principles apply to every avenue of life.

Every person should be aware of their leadership potential and how exercising good leadership is valuable in every role. Whether you are in charge, are serve in a support role, everyone leads in some way. You are either contributing positive leadership or negative. Your life is an influence on someone.

A humorous picture on a calendar showed a sinking ship and stated, "Some people's lives serve no other purpose than to be a warning to others."

The opposite is just as true. Indeed some people serve as an example of consequences, but each person has the potential to show how true confidence provides true leadership, regardless of the role we find ourselves in.

You are a leader. Let's explore how to bring out your leadership skills so your life can be a beacon that guides others – even those above you.

Cultivate an Secure Identity

Bad leadership is almost always born out of insecurity. The person who tests the wind and rushes to the front of the mob is insecure. The person who brow-beats everyone into submission is insecure. The hot-tempered boss is insecure. The bossy personality is also insecure. Arrogance, timidity, abuse, and the enabler are all rooted in insecurity.

Insecurity has many symptoms, but the same root cause. The braggart and know-it-all comes across as proud, but in reality they are trying to make up for their lack of confidence by projecting a proud image.

The person who apologizes for everything or becomes a people pleaser is also insecure. There are healthy ways of pleasing people, but there are also those who wrap up their identity in how they are accepted by others. They will hurt themselves in order to please others because to be rejected is crushing to their identity.

The truth is, every person has insecurities. Some people mask their fears in ways that masquerade as confidence, but at the heart of each person is the same need. "I need to feel valued, accepted, and loved." Even the bitter person who drives everyone away from them is crying out for value, acceptance, and love. They simply do not know how to express this need in healthy ways.

Why do we lose our tempers? At the heart of human wrath is fear. We are afraid of losing control. A fragile ego interprets this as a loss of self-value. We feel violated, so we don't feel loved or self-worth. The human nature way of dealing with this is to regain control of others and circumstances, and wrath is our method of using force to regain control.

The most important part of good leadership is a sense of security in yourself. A great irony is that this cannot be found by feeding self. Consider the wise words of **Proverbs 11:24-25**

> 24 There is *one* who scatters, yet increases more; And there is *one* who withholds more than is right, But it *leads* to poverty.
> 25 The generous soul will be made rich, And he who waters will also be watered himself.

Nowhere is this more true than in human relationships. The person who needs respect tries to get it by demanding respect. People use many destructive methods to force others to respect them, but fear never produces respect. It can force compliance, but the moment someone can break free, they will betray the person controlling them.

Think about the gang lifestyle of today, and the same mentality during the mob era of the 1920s. Mob leaders demanded respect, but how many crime lords ended up dead in the streets? How many gangsters make it to retirement today? The word 'respect' is thrown around a lot, but it isn't respect, but fear. And once the oppressed person has the opportunity to escape, they do so. Or in the crime world, once the underling has the opportunity to kill someone above them, they do so and then they demand to be respected. And the cycle continues.

This is not respect. It doesn't work in the underworld, and it won't work in your relationships. Human nature says, "You will respect me," and then the person living by human nature tries to meet their emotional needs by force.

There is a better way. In fact, there is only one way to find what we are looking for. The person who needs respect gains it by giving it to others. The one who needs to be valued can only find it by valuing others. The writer of Proverbs offers another piece to this puzzle. Look at **Ecclesiastes 11:1**

> Cast your bread upon the waters, For you will find it after many days.

Life doesn't have many instant fixes. True leadership is often cast aside because it takes time to build relationships. But the difference between solid relationships and quick fixes is clearly seen in life. Quick fixes have little lasting value. They must be reapplied perpetually, and false leadership can only remain as long as the ability to strong-arm others remains intact. These relationships are fragile, and it doesn't take much stress to bring them down.

Have you witnessed a winter storm? I live in the South, and the Georgia Pines grow very fast and very tall. They are also fragile. Though they outgrow

Cultivate an Secure Identity

oak trees by far, they have a very short lifespan. There are no hundred-year old Georgia Pines. The south does not get many winter storms, but when they arrive, the first trees to come down is the pines. They snap as soon as ice begins to build up.

Rarely does a solid oak break under freezing weather. They grow slow and steady. It's not uncommon to see oak trees that are more than a hundred years old. Fairly common are the two-hundred year old trees. They withstand because they are built on deep roots and solid wood. It takes time for hardwoods to grow.

Good leadership is also grown slow and steady. It takes time to build relationships and grow respect. Respect grows, not by forcing others to show respect, but by you respecting others. As you cast the bread of good will to others onto the waters of life, after many days it will return to you. The person who waters will be watered. The person who takes will come to poverty. They will have emotional poverty, will starve for love, and will lack self-worth. Then the process of taking will continue, for as they take, they starve, and as they starve, they are driven to take more.

There is a deep truth missing in most people's lives. Self-security is not found in seeking self. While the principle of giving to build relationships works for everyone, the Christian has an advantage that no other person has. Their security is not found in self, but by trusting in the love God has for them.

If your identity is wrapped in how others view you, how others encourage you, accept you, or what people do for you, your life will remain on a tottering foundation. When your peers disrespect you, self will be threatened and anger, bitterness, and frustration will be cultivated in your heart. When your children reject you, it will be a threat. A manager will feel threatened when a team member bad mouths or speaks out.

The more your self-worth is wrapped up in your identity, the more true leadership is undermined, and the more you will feel the need to protect your reputation and sense of self-worth.

The opposite is true for the Christian. Or at least it should be true for the Christian. Like all people living in a body of flesh, Christians are also tempted to look to the flesh to meet their needs. However, not one person on earth can meet your needs. If you are dependent upon affirmation of others, you will always struggle. If you depend on a spouse, child, coworker, friend, pastor, congregation, or any other person to meet your needs, frustration and disappointment are a guarantee.

You can't meet your own needs. How is it fair to put that burden on another person? And the other person is in your same circumstance. They are trying to fulfill those same needs in their own life. You are committing an injustice to others when you put the burden of your satisfaction in life upon their performance.

The same is true when others put that burden on you. You cannot bear that burden, and the quicker you can set a proper expectation in the other person, the quicker healthy relationship building can begin.

Let me share a few passages of scripture that reveal how you become fulfilled and secure in life. From this position of strength, you will have the ability to become a healthy leader to others. First look at **Psalm 36:7-9**

> [7] How precious *is* Your lovingkindness, O God! Therefore the children of men put their trust under the shadow of Your wings.
> [8] They are abundantly satisfied with the fullness of Your house, And You give them drink from the river of Your pleasures.
> [9] For with You *is* the fountain of life; In Your light we see light.

There is only one source of satisfaction. Everything we bring into our own lives is limited at best. The person who fills their life with the pursuit of pleasure is never satisfied. The best they can hope for is a moment of perceived satisfaction, but when the moment has passed, the need for fulfillment arises again. Then internal poverty emerges and becomes a black hole that only grows deeper as we feed it.

The Lord has promised that when He fulfills us, no sorrow comes with that fulfillment. Those who trust in Him as their provider and the source of satisfaction will receive. Not only does God promise to satisfy, but He abundantly satisfies. It overflows from our lives and into others.

When Jesus met the woman at the well, He spoke to her need. She came to the well for water, but Jesus exposed a greater hunger. "You have had five husbands," Jesus told her, "and the man you are now living with is not your husband." She had spent her life trying to fill the emptiness inside by taking from others through relationships. Each one failed and she moved on to the next one. Six intimate relationships failed to meet her need because she was looking to others. Jesus gave her the answer. "I will give you living water." He then went on to explain that the water He will give will not only satisfy her, but will become a spring that pours out of her life and into others.

This has always been the message of God's promise. Look at the promise of **Proverbs 14:14**

> The backslider in heart will be filled with his own ways, But a good man *will be satisfied* from above.

Wow! Do you see the power of this promise? The person trying to fulfill himself never finds satisfaction. They are trying to press ahead in life, but instead of gaining ground, they keep sliding backwards. The more they use their own ways to seek satisfaction, the farther they slip away from it. But the one who looks to God's provision has the promise of satisfaction.

Nothing you can bring into your own life can bring fulfillment. A starving soul can never rise up to become a leader, for they are trying to find their own way — and a person with unmet needs will become a drain on others instead of an inspiration. Let's go deeper into the only source of true satisfaction. Look now at **1 John 4:16**

> And we have known and believed the love that God has for us. God is love, and he who abides in love abides in God, and God in him.

Do you believe in the love God has for you? Most people do not. Most Christians do not grasp the depth of God's love. Look around. God has designed everything in life for your good. Though sin has corrupted this world, it does not change the depth of God's love. Most of us have heard Romans 8:28, "All things work together for the good of those who love God and are called into His purpose."

Even hardship is designed to drive you into the love of God. Without a failing world system, we would never have the longing of our hearts to seek the satisfaction that only comes through the love of God. The person who abides in God's love is the receiver of God's satisfaction. When He is your exceedingly great reward, everything will have the right perspective, and satisfaction is a guarantee.

The person who learns to trust in God's provision, receives all things and becomes the leader who can give to others. As long as your life is focused on gratifying your needs, life will be focused on finding satisfaction instead of fulfilling your purpose in His calling. Finally, let's look at **Isaiah 58:10-12**

> [10] *If* you extend your soul to the hungry And satisfy the afflicted soul, Then your light shall dawn in the darkness, And your darkness shall *be* as the noonday.
> [11] The LORD will guide you continually, And satisfy your soul in drought, And strengthen your bones; You shall be like a watered garden, And like a spring of water, whose waters do not fail.

This is leadership. Do you see the common theme of all these passages? Satisfaction comes from above. The one who is satisfied in the Lord is then called to become the flow of God's love toward others. The New Testament teaches that once we have received from God, we then comfort others with what God has given us. We first become receivers of God's love and benefits, then we become leaders who give to others out of the overflow of our own hearts. Then God rewards us for giving to others what we have received, and then we are given all the more.

True leadership can work no other way. When our soul is in poverty, we become takers of others. When our soul is abounding with the satisfaction that can only come from above, we become instruments of good to others. We can then lead others with a clear purpose. Once we are confident in our identity in Christ and confident in the love God has for us, we can then have confidence as we lead others by either example, instruction, or both.

The established heart has the power to lead. The hungry soul cannot. At least not in a healthy and effective way. Leadership should never leave wounded people in its wake. True leadership will build up others so they either are encouraged by our support, support our calling, or go out into their own calling with tools we encouraged them to develop.

We are receivers from above. We are to cast what we have into the lives of others. As what we invest into others matures, it returns to us in healthy relationships, respect of others, common goals and values, and many other fruitful ways.

Leadership begins with you establishing your own heart, and from a firm foundation, your leadership will emerge to fulfill the calling you have been given. This is true for both the extrovert and the introvert, the leader of others and the supporter of others.

Self-centeredness dies when satisfaction comes from above. A secure person will have the confidence to lead, and the ability to use leadership to equip others instead of taking from them. We should be reaping the fruit of the investment of ourselves in people – not sapping the life out of them. Be a cultivator instead of a strip-miner.

Tale of Two Leaders

Most people rise to the level of the perception of others. When someone feels they are valued and a leader believes in them, they perform at a higher level. A person who feels the weight of others looking down on them will have a difficult time performing, for they feel as if the deck is stacked against them. This is true even if this is their perception and not reality. Perception is reality to the person behind it.

One of the challenges of leadership is to overcome negative perceptions and get others to adopt a positive perspective. When someone feels valued, they will take ownership in the mission. Leadership is teaching others how to become established in their own sense of worth, and to value their contribution to the team's effort.

Let's consider the contrast between two managers in the same company – Steve and Jeff. Steve always had a positive attitude. He managed a branch for a distribution company, and this division grew. Each person had a good attitude and company morale was good. When a new delivery driver was hired, Steve came back to check on how he was doing.

"Paul is doing a great job, isn't he?" Steve asked the warehouse manager. Several workers were nearby and they all looked at Paul.

"Yes, he's doing great."

Steve's question accomplished two important things. The way he worded it set a positive expectation. The manager looked at Paul's performance with the expectation of finding something good. The peers of Paul looked at him with the perception of comradery and as a welcomed contributor to the team. Paul heard the question and felt good about his role, while also feeling that he was a valued part of the team.

That one question, worded in a positive way, created a positive perception for everyone, and it created the desire in Paul to live up to Steve's positive expectation. The only way Paul could have felt the pressure of measuring up would be if he was already unmotivated and just looking for a paycheck without merit. Those people exist, but they are not as common as we might think. Most people underperform because they lose hope; not because they don't care.

Paul succeeded.

A few years later, Steve was promoted to the corporate office, and Jeff was promoted to branch manager. These two men were polar opposites. Jeff was very critical and demanding. What's more, Jeff did not acknowledge performance or reward hard work. He expected more. If someone performed, the expectation was increased.

Another delivery driver was hired, Tom. A few days later, Jeff walked back to check up on him. "Do you think this guy is going to work out? I have a lot of other people who applied. If someone isn't performing, let's cut them and move on to someone else."

How was Tom viewed by his peers? The warehouse manager looked at Tom with a critical eye, trying to think whether Tom had shown any signs of failure. Tom's coworkers looked at him and evaluated his worth to be on the team. In a single moment, Tom felt the weight of the world on his shoulders. Not only was he trying to learn a new job, but he now had to fight an uphill battle to prove his value. Before getting off the starting line, Tom already had the perception that he was losing the race.

Within a few months, morale in the warehouse plummeted, employees felt the burden of measuring up to a standard that seemed unattainable, and teamwork began to crumble. Instead of reaching for the company vision, each person spent time complaining about the company, the workload, favoritism, and the lack of recognition.

A long time employee said, "Why should I be killing myself with these impossible shipping deadlines?" He pointed toward the office, "No one up there cares about me or sees what I do, so what difference does it make?"

Do you see the difference between these two scenarios? This is not a hypothetical scenario, but was an actual event. This is also played out in companies all over the world, and in homes all over the world.

When children lose hope in pleasing their parents, or feel they cannot measure up to what they consider as unreasonable expectations, they give up. Rebellion is often the fruit of discouragement.

How do you think Jeff responded to the loss of productivity? He took a strong-armed approach as he demanded more productivity. He fired employees, and even more quit. The new people hired could not possibly outperform those who had once created the company's fastest growing branch. They were entering an arena where they could not win. Then the company became a rotating door, and would remain this way until either management changed, or current management wizened up and took on a better approach.

Leaders who see control slipping away have a tendency to use the same failing methods, but with a bigger hammer. This is true in each leadership role – corporate management, church leadership, and parenting. When those under the leader are not acting as expected, the fallback solution is to employ threats instead of cultivating the people under leadership. Certainly there is a time for corrective action through punishment/discipline, but punishment is not the fix-all band aid people seem to think it is.

The short-term easier solution is to drop back and punt. Get rid of the problem is the easier way, but it never fixes the problem. The goal of every leader should be to develop future leaders. To cultivate someone to the point where they value what is right creates a strong family, church, or work unit, and the only way to succeed is to take difficulties and use them as learning experiences.

Sometimes that learning experience is for you, the leader. One of my greatest leadership lessons came when I was eighteen years old. I had a controlling attitude. The world had to be ordered, or I had to fix it. As a summer job I took on a babysitting role to make extra money. That's when I met the destroyer of babysitters.

After I started, it was revealed that I was the third keeper of the destroyer this year. The first two had quit. The one before me got so angry that he stomped off the job, leaving the kids alone. The destroyer had a name – Johnny. Johnny taught me more about leadership than any book could have ever done. He was strong-willed and one of the worst Type-A personalities I have ever met.

The first day on the job, Johnny challenged everything I said. He didn't have to do what I said. He had his own way. Add to this, his personality clashed with mine. Everything he did seemed to get on my nerves. Most was probably intentional. I met Johnny head on, and when he pushed my buttons, I tried to force submission – mostly by banning him to his room.

Everyday brought on more punishment for Johnny. One time I told him I wouldn't take him off restriction until he could keep his smart mouth shut for an hour. I think Johnny watched the clock, for a few times he made it to fifty-five minutes, and then he would shout his rebellion at the door. I'd reset the clock, and Johnny would almost make it again before having a new meltdown. All he had to do was keep his remarks to himself for one hour, but he refused to do it. He would rather continue punishment than to give in to the battle of the wills.

Every day was a miserable experience. I'd leave stressed out. He would be stressed out. The moment he heard his parents pull into the driveway he'd yell, "You're not the boss anymore," and he'd go wild.

It was about two months into our conflict and Johnny lost all restraint. He reached the point where he felt no hope and completely rebelled. All chaos broke loose and both of us had the worse day of our lives. He had a total meltdown. Mr. Controller had met Captain Resistor, and we discovered how nuclear fission was achieved.

I went home that night and contemplated the disastrous events of the day. No matter what I did, I simply could not control this monster of a child. Then something in my understanding dawned and I realized that my role was not to control him. My role was to lead him, not force him. Instead of boundaries, I had put him into shackles, and instead of guiding him into the boundaries of what was required, I was chasing him with a stick (not literally) to brow beat him back into submission. I was requiring Johnny to act in a way that he was not capable of acting. I was trying to conform him to my will instead of nurturing him into a way of thinking that would give him ownership of his behavior.

As a parent of five children, I can see how these same principles apply to varying personality types. I didn't know there were five opposites until I had my fifth child. Not one of them can be put into a box without smothering them. One child can be instructed and respond willingly, while others do not respond as easily. Firm words will make one child stop and listen, but will cause another to crumble under its weight. There is not a cookie cutter approach, for each person must be evaluated and approached with a different method.

It's not easy to effectively evaluate each person. This is why relationship building is important in leadership. The quicker someone can be nurtured into self-management, the quicker we will all have rest. With Johnny, it was a matter of pride. His rebellion was considered a threat to my sense of self-value. When he rejected my instructions, it was a threat to my ego. Once my ego was no longer the focus, the real issue could be addressed.

True leadership stands or falls based on how we deal with conflict. When the conflict becomes about me verses you, I am no longer leading. The moment I must defend my reputation or feelings, I am no longer leading. It's not a leader's job to protect their reputation by any other means than by living out what they say they believe. Even slander cannot destroy a reputation for long – unless we allow it to derail us into a battle of the wills.

Leadership is not based on emotions, but rather on what is truly valued. Conflict reveals whether we value our principles or our self-centered desires. The one who is established in the truth that satisfaction is from above will be able to handle conflict based on what is right and not based on self-preservation.

This is why cultivating both relationships and a secure identity is essential for good leadership. It's a hard lesson to learn, but once it becomes reality, it will change the way you approach conflict and how you cultivate people with difficult personalities.

Those who care more about their self-interest than they care about the person or people they are leading have already lost focus on the mission. When someone learns to value people, they will discover that some of the people who others would have pushed aside will become some of the best leaders. A person who is cultivated out of challenges will have a stronger perspective than others. These are your best allies waiting to be discovered.

In the next chapter, we'll discuss how to work through conflicts. In this chapter it's important to understand this main point. People tend to rise to the level of your faith in them. It's not only important for you to believe in them, but you need to find ways to communicate this to them.

Perception is reality in the eyes of each individual. A leader can have complete faith in their subordinates, peers, or family, but if that person feels you don't trust or value them, they will respond as if you are their critic.

Let me give an important piece of advice that applies to both leaders of people and leaders in support roles. Never publically devalue another person, and always seize the opportunity to publically affirm others. A leader should avoid criticizing someone in front of others – even if they deserve it. Wait for the opportunity to meet out of the focus of the group when a fault needs to be addressed.

Always sandwich criticism between slices of praise. As a manager, I've often had to take employees into corrective action. The corrective action is the criticism, but it's important to begin with affirming their value and focusing on something they are doing right. Then move to corrective action, and end with affirmation of their qualities. Explain how corrective action is necessary in order to consistently adhere to company policies among all employees. The goal is to give employees the opportunity to correct the areas where they fell short so their strengths can shine. Then end by pointing out some of their strengths.

If criticism isn't sandwiched between praise, the employee will assume management is fault-finding with the goal of getting rid of them. I have found that when I make it clear that I believe in them and that my goal is for them to succeed, employees respond better. Some personalities require corrective action before they take criticism seriously, yet the goal is not to find a way to eliminate them from the team. If someone perceives that management is against them, corrective action has a negative effect. If they believe you are pulling for their success, an employee will usually make changes.

Don't give up on a struggling employee. You'll be surprised at how many times a person can excel once they understand your faith in them. Knowing you are partnering with them for their success can change everything. A little grace goes a long way.

If you are growing your own leadership in a support role, it is equally important to apply these same principles from a subordinate perspective. Never publicly criticize your manager. This is true even if they are not present. Many comments will bleed through the grapevine, and negative comments always sound worse when repeated by others. Always publicly support a manager, even if you don't agree with a decision he or she makes.

Some people consider this sucking up, but there is a better reason for this. This is not saying we praise every decision and make it look like we agree with everything. It's possible to support management without agreeing with their decisions.

When a manager knows you are supportive publically, it opens the door to speak candidly in private. The goal is to present ideas from the 'frontline' perspective. A good idea goes a lot farther than the criticism of a bad idea. People become defensive when the only communication they hear is criticism. When a manager perceives you are supporting their goals, they will be more receptive of questioning a decision with new ideas. Once again, from a manager's perspective I can say, "Don't tell me what's wrong. Tell me what you think will make it better." Don't launch complaints. Present ideas.

Your goal as a leader is not only to communicate the vision of where you are going, but also the vision of what you see in the other person. They need to hear you say to others, "I believe in this person." They need to hear you say, "You are valued." Sometimes this needs to be communicated in verbal affirmations. Sometimes this needs to be communicated without words. It must be a constant communication.

One of the realities of human nature is that most people fill in the silent gaps with misassumptions. What is not spoken is often interpreted as disapproval. Have you ever had someone say that you are mad when you had no reason to be angry? Have you ever assumed someone was ignoring you out of spite, anger, or disapproval? For some reason humanity tends to fill in silence with false assumptions. And these assumptions are almost always negative – and wrong.

The more you communicate affirmation to others, the more they will rise to meet the self-image they perceive in your eyes. The less they feel affirmed, the more they will be discouraged. With discouragement comes discontentment, bitterness, and frustration. Perception is reality; therefore, perception must be shaped through leadership.

If you teach people that you believe in them, they will believe in themselves, and they will believe in you and the common goals you share.

Stop trying to make others believe in you. This method of leadership rarely works. Believe in others. Make them believe in themselves. That is the goal of leadership. From here, everything else will begin falling into place.

Discovering the Positive You

Each person carries emotional baggage. It's the invisible bag on your back where you store wrongs, hurts, and frustrations. Every offense is a stone you must deal with. Most stones are tiny, but even grains of sand, if gathered in quantity, becomes a heavy weight.

Little annoyances may be grains of sand, perceived and real wrongs may be small rocks, and deep wounds and hurts are heavy boulders. Regardless of the size of our baggage's content, it all becomes heavy to carry.

People have a hard time removing their baggage. Sometimes we feel we have the right to carry the weight. In truth, we do have this right, but our reasoning is flawed. We carry the weight as though we are holding others accountable, but we are the ones bearing the penalty.

Take deep wounds as an example. A person who has been deeply wounded usually carries the heavy boulder of that wound on their back. It then sabotages future relationships and crushes the person's ability to thrive in a relationship. People may say, "Let go of the past and move on," but often the answer is, "I can't let it go."

The wounded person clings to the heavy weight as though the hurt is more valuable than the freedom without it. It is very difficult to let go of wrongs – even when we can see it destroying our peace, freedom, and self-worth.

It's not only deep wounds that sabotage our lives, but also the little stones and grains of sand. It takes longer to build up the weight, but everyone who holds on to wrongs will accumulate stress. This affects how they relate to others and it takes a toll on their own emotional health.

Let me share a lesson I learned from managing a call center. This life application can be applied to each scenario of living where people interact.

To make this scenario applicable to the reader, I'm going to put you into the seat of a struggling employee. You have been dealing with a lot of people today. Some of them have difficult personalities. Many of them aren't listeners and haven't followed your basic instructions. By the end of the day, you are feeling frustrated. Add to this, the last few weeks and months are also weighing on you. The same annoyances keep being repeated and you are wondering why people can't get it. As the stress slowly builds, you begin getting snappy at customers. Add to this, you are having trouble getting along with a coworker, and have about had it with everything.

As a manager, I've noticed these things and have tried to coach you, but things continue to go downhill. Now I'm going to sit down with you to work through these issues.

The first thing I want you to do is take your focus off what frustrates you and do a personal inventory. Write down on a piece of paper the positive attributes that are part of your life. Then write down the positive attributes you want to bring out in your life – the things that are important that you want to become. Here are some examples:

I am joyful
I am happy
I am kind to others
I want to be patient
I want to have peace
I want to show love

The Bible says, "As a man thinks in his heart, so is he." I have yet to meet a person who says, "I want to be hateful," or desires to become things that are negative. We all want to bring out our best, but we often don't know how to do this.

Look at your list – both categories. This is who you are as a person. These are the attributes of your character and the real you. The problems you carry are not you, but are the things that are burying you.

Now take small pieces of paper. I like to use post-it notes. Write down the things that trouble you. Be as general or specific as you want. Here are some examples:

I am angry
I get frustrated
This customer called me an idiot
My spouse is demanding
My kids are ungrateful
I can't control my temper

Take as many pieces of paper as you feel is necessary to express your frustrations. Then take each paper and lay them one at a time on your list of positive attributes. This is how life works. Frustrations rob you of joy because you place them over joy to block this out of your life. Impatience buries patience. Anger buries your peace. Resentment buries your love.

The things you allow to take up residence in your life are crowding out who you are as a person. These things must be removed in order to reveal the attributes of your life you desire.

How much greater does this truth apply to the Christian life. According to Galatians 5, the Holy Spirit within you bears this fruit:

Love
Joy
Peace
Patience
Kindness
Goodness
Faith
Gentleness
Self-control

When who we are in the Spirit has the freedom to grow, this is the natural result of the Christian life. You don't produce these things. None of these are produced by your works, efforts, or accomplishments. It is the natural process of a fruitful life. But why don't these things emerge. Just before the fruit of the Spirit is explained, the scriptures explain the harmful works of the flesh. Most of the things that plague everyday life is found in the works of the flesh: hatred, outbursts of wrath, contentions, jealousy, selfishness, and divisions (i.e. broken relationships).

These are the things that prevent the fruit of the Spirit from emerging in your life. You have to do nothing to make fruit grow – except weed the garden of your life to remove the things that choke out your life and prevent these things from flourishing.

If you are bitter, love is choked. Not only is love choked, but so is peace, joy, patience, and every part of life that has true value. Anger chokes out these things and produces its works – wrath, jealousy, and contentions. Then peace, love, joy, and every valuable part of life is also choked. The things that produce harmful works must be weeded out before the garden of your soul can flourish.

When emotions run out of control, and the works of the flesh fill your life, ridding these things may seem like a daunting task, but the solution is much less complicated than you might imagine.

If you look at the problems of life as a mountain of trouble, life can appear hopeless. If you have an out of control temper or other issue, it can appear impossible to conquer. However, if you open your emotional baggage and take out one stone at a time, it doesn't take long to begin seeing progress.

And this is how we are going to approach frustration in your job.

As an example, let's look at the buildup of frustration with the customers our team faced. Why are you, the employee, having more trouble with customers at 5 p.m. than you had at 8 a.m.? Why was it easier two months ago than it is today? The reason is because you are carrying stones of frustration gathered throughout the day into the conversation with the customer at 5. You are not merely dealing with this customer, but you are borrowing frustration from all the customers who came beforehand. Then it is impossible to deal with the person on the phone with you based on the situation at hand. You will react (or should I say 'overreact') to that customer based on the baggage you're carrying at that moment.

Why do you overreact to your spouse or kids, or read negativity into a situation where one may not have existed? You are reacting to the baggage you are carrying, and not merely to the situation at hand. What's more, you will feel justified and the other will feel violated. Then they will react to match the negative energy you are projecting. When they react negatively, you will feel affirmed in your negative assumption, and the tension will continue to build.

Identifying the problem is important, but now let's look at how we can overcome our perceptions and learn how to deal with frustrations and stress in a healthy way.

Unloading the Burden

This is where the rubber meets the road. Each person has the ability to deal with stress in a healthy way. When we fail to do so, we add stress to our burden, and over time it builds up. Because most of us have grown accustomed to enduring stress, we become desensitized to it, and over time become unaware of its presence in our lives. We only see the symptoms of stress and mistake the symptom as the problem.

We think we are impatient, but the truth is that impatience is a symptom of the burden of stress. We think our spouse is driving us crazy, but the root of the problem is the heavy burden of stress. We walked with a stoop under its weight, but because this has become the norm, we overlook the heavy burden and zero in on an isolated irritation that has our attention at that moment. And we react from our reserve of stress, so our reaction is disproportionate to the offense.

Have you witnessed two people who can't get along? As an outside observer, we are amazed that two people can go into a heated conflict over such petty problems. And sometimes we don't even see a problem. The two warriors do. They may be arguing about who always gets the last soda in the fridge, but they are reacting to years of pent up frustration that is being dumped into their emotions at the moment of conflict.

There are clues to this reality. "You always..." "You never..." "You just think..." "You are just doing this because..."

The phrase 'you always' is clear evidence this person is drawing from the past and throwing it into the present. "You just think," tells us the person is taking their emotional assumptions and projecting it onto the other person. Then they are not reacting to the situation at hand, but to the emotional energy being drawn from pent up stress. If I am stressed out, my feelings must be what you are thinking, is the assumption. And that assumption is almost always false. However, to the emotionally charged person, it is reality.

This is why people have such a difficult time resolving conflict. The greater problem is found in their baggage, but because they are demanding resolution from the person they are targeting, a solution is hard to find. The other person not only has to agree that they are wrong in the conflict at hand, but they also must accept responsibility for the other person's feelings.

There are times when the other party agrees to take the blame, but this will not resolve the breakdown. One person feels unfairly blamed, and the other still carries the baggage that created the overreaction. Over time bitterness will grow on both sides. Most people will not accept the blame being placed on them, so the best they can hope for is a temporary ceasefire.

The person in which you have conflict is not your problem. Even if someone is hard to get along with, they still are not your problem. If someone commits the same offense every time you cross paths, they are still not your problem. The burden on your back is the problem.

If you deal with frustration in healthy ways, every offense is the first offense. If you are dealing with customers, each customer's problem is a new event and even if it's the tenth time you've had to address this today, it's still the first time. If this isn't true for your life, you are carrying yesterday's stress into today, and stress will continue to grow.

Long-term stress creates damaged emotions, and it takes a toll on your physical health as well. It's time to start picking the rocks out of the baggage and removing the burdens that sabotage your life.

Let's look at a scenario that is common in daily family life. Mom and daughter are arguing. What do you suppose will be in every verbal altercation? "You never," and "You always." Mom gets frustrated at having to deal with her daughter and she thinks back to all the times her expectations were not met. "You are always disrespectful." "You never do your chores." "I always have to tell you…"

What would happen if she found herself in conflict, but could stay focused on the situation at hand without drawing from the past? She could remain focused on the mission before her, and it would be easier to keep her emotions in check. If her daughter smarted off, she could focus on how that specific incident is not acceptable, and would have a better chance at a controlled resolution.

This is where we must learn to compartmentalize our offenses. You may have heard it is hypocrisy to compartmentalize your life, but this is not so when it comes to stress and offenses. Each frustration must be made to stand alone and then dealt with as an isolated incident.

Forty-nine times in the New Testament the Bible deals with the topic of forgiveness. When it comes to our lives, God deals with our mistakes as they occur. God has given us an example by saying things like, "I cast your sins into the sea of forgetfulness," and, "I remove your sins as far as the east is from the west."

The person laden with guilt has the misconception that God is keeping a log of wrongs and when we blow it, God is going to say, "This is the 253rd time you've done this." The reality is, every time is the first time. We blow it, and God works to get us back into a correct mindset so we don't miss out on the good things He has for us. We are the list keepers, not God. What's more, God is constantly reiterating the need for us to trust in His love and forgiveness as He calls us to discard our lists of guilt.

We see how Jesus taught us the need to adopt the same process of forgiveness. The culture of that day lived by the Old Testament principle, an eye for an eye. Peter got a noble idea that he presented to Jesus. "What if I forgive people who sin against me seven times?" Seven whole times! That is seven times more than the cultural standard.

Jesus put this into a whole new perspective. "Don't just forgive seven times. I say that you should forgive seventy times seven times."

Everyone can remember seven offenses, but no one can remember four-hundred and ninety offenses. Even if I forgive with sincerity, I can still remember seven offenses back. God's method is to place our record-keeping out of reach. Unless I am not forgiving other people and keeping a record, I can never remember that many specific offenses; therefore, the message is for us to take our lead from God's method and put every offense into the sea of forgetfulness. Then every offense is the first time.

This is a hard truth to live by. Something within our ego says, "Forgiveness will allow this person to get away with a wrong." This is a lie. Forgiveness breaks your bondage to that wrong. Each time you are offended (intentionally or unintentionally), you must take a moment to self-evaluate and take that stone and drop it. The person who committed the offense is not burdened when you hold to the offense. You are paying a perpetual penalty for holding on to what you dislike. It is your stress you are releasing when you refuse to carry that burden.

You must evaluate what is valuable in your life. Do you value the stone of offense more than your peace, joy, and happiness? If so, you will place that stone in your baggage and forfeit the joys of life.

Your ego will remind you of the offense and demand you pick up the stones – even after you have released them. At that moment, you must refuse to do so. Otherwise it will be a burden on your back again. When the next offense comes, you will be tempted to revisit the rubble, but if you do, instead of resolving conflict, you will stoop with the weight of everything you pick up again.

Keep in mind that you have a lifetime of habit to overcome. Human nature loves to cling to what we hate. It is irrational, but true. As you put absolute forgiveness into practice, you'll establish the habit of forgiveness and then the desire to reacquire the offenses of the past will fade.

Each time you feel frustrated, take a moment to evaluate what you value in life. Do you want to keep living a life of victimhood? Or do you want to cultivate a healthy life of joy? Look at your life. Does bitterness ever produce satisfaction in any form?

This goes back to our personal inventory. Look at who you are without these burdens. This is your goal. The only thing between you and that goal is the negativity you harbor. It blocks out who you are and what you desire for your life and attitude.

As you journey through life, the burdens on your back will emerge and call for your attention. This is your opportunity to deal with that offense and cast it out of your life. If you do so, over time the load will become lighter and you'll root out the weeds crowding your life.

Conflict is inevitable. When conflict comes, refuse to allow your emotions to grab the stones of the past and bring them into the conflict. Deal with each circumstance as something which stands alone and must be resolved based on what you value in life. As a leader, the goal is to nurture others into maturity, valuing a common goal, and seeing the worth of a healthy attitude.

If you deal with conflict based on emotional baggage, the goal of what you hope to resolve will be lost. Never battle your assumptions in the other person. Never battle your emotions in the other person. Never use your emotions to beat someone into submission. Ride your emotions when they support your passions, but subdue them when they attempt to rule your life.

When we deal with each conflict based on its own worth, we can resolve things in healthy ways. Or we can walk away from the lack of resolution with a clear understanding of what the issue is. The words 'always' and 'never' do not belong in our conflicts. Yesterday's stress does not belong to today. Previous customers or people you have dealt with do not belong in your communication with the current person you are dealing with.

Each negative feeling must be evaluated, resolved when a resolution is possible, and cast out of your life as quickly as possible. Every time must be the first time. Anything else becomes a burden of stress on your back.

Leading Out of Conflict

Until now, the main focus of this book has been on you, the leader. Learning how to manage yourself is crucial in the quest to effectively manage others. In daily life in work, family, or other organization, conflicts are inevitable. There are times when you will need to lead two people out of conflict and into a healthy working relationship.

When two people are in conflict, management falls into chaos and it can seem like fires of anger are erupting faster than they can be put out. When you get one person under control, the other is still in combat mode. No sooner do you squelch one person's emotions before the other person reignites the conflict with their emotions.

It isn't possible to force someone into a wise standard of behavior, but there are methods you can use to take their focus off of their ego and onto the circumstance at the heart of the conflict. When managing conflict, the worst option is to get frustrated and jump in with your own emotions.

Each person must buy into the value of the goal, and desire it more than their ego. No one likes to think of themselves as egotistical, but we all are to varying degrees. Ego is just another word for our perception of self-worth. I want to be valued. If my sense of value is threatened, my first reaction is to defend myself.

This is why this book began by learning how to establish a sense of self-value on a better foundation than emotions and flawed perceptions. The person who is secure in their sense of self-worth can withstand criticism and offenses much easier than the one who has a fragile sense of self-worth. At the heart of most defensive reactions and outburst of anger is a threatened ego.

The first step in resolving conflict – especially an ongoing and growing conflict – is to teach each individual how to understand their own emotions and how to find self-worth outside of the conflict. Once the threat to ego has been removed, most conflicts will resolve themselves. The more fragile a person's self-worth becomes, the more reactive they will be. The stronger a person's sense of self-worth, the harder it is to threaten their ego. As we grow into maturity, we learn to stop depending on the affirmation of others. We also learn how to shrug off the comments and actions that once would have sent us into defensive mode. Consider the wise words of **Proverbs 18:19**

> A brother offended *is harder to win* than a strong city, And contentions *are* like the bars of a castle.

While someone is in offended mode, winning them over to a position or good course of action is nearly impossible. It's easier for an army to defeat a city in war than to win over an ego defending itself. Arguments almost never end with both sides agreeing. One side may grow tired of fighting and concede the effort, but even if they concede their position verbally, they will be reluctant to support the other person's position. In their heart, they are still offended and they will do little to support the victor. Many times they are merely regrouping, and the next battle will have more emotional reactions and greater resistance.

Before constructive dialog can begin, the emotions must first be disarmed and then the person will have the ability to listen. Until then, the person isn't listening to the opposing point; they are waiting for a pause so they can counter argue. Or they will try to overrun the discussion with louder words.

The problem with resolving conflict is that we try to force the other to listen to reasoning while emotions are ruling the mind. If we are in the argument, we may be focused on our point, but our emotions are blinding us to anything but the principle we feel strongly about.

Let me point out another common flaw in reasoning here. Many times we say, "It's the principle of the matter," that we are forcing. I've seen people in a heated conflict over something that has no value whatsoever. But they will not allow the issue to drop because of the 'principle of the matter.' Do you know what that principle is? It is that 'self' has been offended, and we aren't going to take a wrong. We aren't fighting because the toilet paper roll is feeding from the top instead of the bottom. We are fighting because we aren't going to let them get away with disregarding our feelings and threatening our sense of self-worth.

This is the heart of almost every heated conflict. One side or the other is not fighting for any other principle than to defend their sense of self-worth. When both sides are fighting for ego's sake, there is no limit to the depth this war can go.

Consider the first murder in the Bible. Cain slew Able, and what was his motivation? His offering was rejected, and this caused him to feel devalued. Then he targeted Able. Able did nothing wrong, but in Cain's mind, his rage was justified. When ego is our principle, irrational anger always feels justifiable.

Cain's issue wasn't his brother. The issue was that Cain needed to rethink his offering to God. A rational mind would have said, "What can I learn from Able? What made his offering good?" But when self-worth became the focus, jealousy and rage took over. Emotions can be great servants, but they are terrible masters. Once emotions rule your life, it can only lead to trouble. If you allow emotions to take control during conflict, it rarely has a good outcome – unless the other person employs methods that effectively diffuses your emotions.

It's a hard position to achieve. We have let emotions rule us for a lifetime. Reprogramming our ways of thinking is hard. Defusing our emotions instead of firing them at the other person is hard. Even harder is defusing the other person's emotions. We are taking someone who is unwilling to subdue their emotions, and even unaware of their emotional state, and we are trying to use methods that will defuse them so we can get to the problem.

Most emotionally charged conflicts have these words:

You never...

You always...

I'm not going to take that...

How dare he/she speak to me that way...

Is a specific problem being addressed with any of these statements? No. The problem is not even on the radar. The problem lit the fuse, but now the explosion of emotions are the focus. People are then focused on their anger toward the other person and not the actual problem.

So how is conflict resolved? There is a two-fold approach. The first effort is to take emotions out of the way so the problem can be brought back into focus. The second issue that must be addressed is to give people the tools to self-manage and prevent emotions from ruling their working relationships with others.

As long as emotional tension exists, a new conflict is one offense away. And when the expectation of offense is present, even innocent comments can be misinterpreted as offensive.

An effective leader needs to take each individual aside and get them to focus on the heart of the issue causing conflict. Sometimes the only real problem is that people are allowing their emotions to rule their minds, and everything is interpreted through whichever emotion is ruling their mind at that time.

Sometimes we have to say, "Here is the problem. Here is what is preventing you from resolving the problem." When all emotion is out of the way, the vast majority of what people fight about appears silly. Why are we fighting about toilet paper? Or the color of the table cloth? Name the conflict. Almost every conflict is an easy resolution – once emotions are handled in healthy ways.

Bottling up emotions isn't the answer. Self-evaluating and dealing with emotions in a healthy way is the answer. I'll say again this basic truth, most emotional reactions emerge from a flawed sense of self-worth. Once someone feels valued, emotions are easy to control. If someone becomes dependent upon affirmation, encouragement, success, or praise in order to feel valued, they will remain on a fragile foundation. Anyone dependent on gaining self-worth from others will always feel threatened when something appears to lessen that sense of value.

A leader must encourage, praise, and affirm others so they understand they are valued, but also they must guide others onto a solid foundation where their sense of value isn't based on achievement or the affirmation of others, but the love of God. Some of these principles can be applied in a non-Christian environment, but only the Christian has the Spirit of God that cries, "Abba Father." We have the understanding that we are valued as God's children, and that our worth isn't based on our performance, but based on the fact that God is love. God doesn't love us because we do good. God loves us because He is love, and love must express itself by loving others. We are loved because He is love. Even when we blow it, God's love remains, and we have self-worth because we know and believe in the love God has for us (1 John 4:16).

Believing in yourself can only take you so far. Believing in yourself because you have been given all things by God takes you out of human limitation. If I have security by trusting in all that God is, and His love and promises toward me, what can you do to rob me of that confidence? Nothing. I can now see your emotional reaction for what it is, and it does not threaten me. I can affirm your feelings as valid, but not react or make decisions based on your or my emotions.

If you are not drawn into the war over emotions, you can remain calm as you help the other person work through their emotions until they are able to refocus on the real issue at hand. Then you can look for the opportunity to show how emotions should be servants. Lead others into gaining a secure sense of self-worth so they can be in control instead of controlled by emotions.

The greatest challenge is when you have to lead two emotionally controlled people out of conflict. Each person is feeding the emotional fire of the other. One is calmed, but the moment they interact again, the fire is reignited. This is when two people must be first dealt with separately, guided into a right way of viewing the problem, and then moderate both into good dialog together. When voices become pitched, it's the first sign of smoke, and the fire can be squelched by refocusing on the two-fold problem. One is the issue causing disagreement; second is the false feelings of a threatened ego (or sense of self-worth).

Let's put this into practice with an illustration. Jane and Susan are employees of mine and are having trouble getting along. They've been bickering for a while, but this isn't unusual for a close working environment. One day the bickering came to a head. Their bickering became heated, and they ended up in a shouting match.

After intervening, the fight ended, both gave each other an angry glare, and they went their separate ways. A couple of days later, they were at each other's throats again. "She always does the easy tasks and leaves everyone else to do the hard things," Jane protested.

Susan returns fire, "You think you can just order me around like you're my boss. If you focused on your own work, you wouldn't have time to lord over everyone else."

The rest of their argument becomes unintelligible because both are trying to talk over the other. As a manager, I couldn't address the problem because once one tried to say something, the other would be inflamed, and vise-versa.

The disagreement didn't start two days ago. The heart of the problem is that neither wants to do the undesirable tasks. When one finds herself in a position where they have to do it, they are angry. If it happens again, not only are they angry for getting stuck with the task, but they are carrying anger from the last time they got stuck with it.

As a manager, I've seen both sides. There are times when someone is trying to avoid work and doesn't carry their fair share. However, often times the employee only notices when they get stuck with an undesirable task. Everyone tries to avoid doing the tasks they hate, but one time I assigned Susan to work it. Another time I assigned a different employee. When it was her turn, I assigned Jane to do it.

She was just as guilty of avoiding the task as Susan, but because she only sees the workload when it falls on her, she assumes she is always the one getting stuck with it. Her personality type has trouble not pointing out when she assumes something is an injustice. Because we are dealing with human nature, most injustices are noticed when it threatens ourselves.

When someone does have a performance issue, managers address the problem, but are not at liberty to discuss personnel matters with other employees. Though corrective action may be running its course, people have the tendency to assume someone is getting away with beating the system.

Most conflicts arise from perception and not reality. People (including ourselves) only see from our point of view. We only see our side of the equation. We fill in the gaps of what we don't see with negative assumptions, and then we treat our flawed perception as though it were reality.

The more we are aware of our own human shortcoming in this area, the more we can diffuse our emotions by recognizing our assumptions may not be reality. As leaders, we need to guide others into this realization as well. In my scenario, I need to show Jane the reality of distributed work, and that each person is doing as she does, pushing off difficult tasks in the hopes someone else will do it out of the goodness of their heart.

Jane needs to be shown that how she approaches Susan determines whether an issue is resolved with or without conflict. Once a relationship has broken down, every comment or question will be interpreted through negative assumptions. If the relationship is healthy, Jane could ask, "Hey Susan. When is the last time you worked on this task?" Then a dialog would be open and both could determine whose turn it is.

If the relationship has already soured, Susan will view the question as an accusation. That's when team building and cooperation needs to be used to restore the relationship. Once there is mutual trust and mutual respect, questions won't be viewed as loaded.

To rebuild the relationship, Jane must buy into the idea of being intentional about showing good faith toward Susan. Susan must do the same. This works best when both are being intentional about cooperation. However, if one is faithfully working toward this goal, acts of goodwill will have a great influence on the other.

When Susan feels accused, she will react with defensiveness and will go into battle mode. When Jane feels slighted, she will become critical toward Susan, and future perceived slights will put her into battle-mode. I say perceived because most offenses are based on perception and are not intentional.

This scenario is played out in relationships every day. It could be the perception of favoritism, the perception of injustice, the perception of manipulation, or it could be a personality conflict. Comments that seem innocent to one person could be viewed as a threat to the other. All it takes to generate conflict is one person hungry for affirmation being perceived as a braggart by the other. Misconceptions appear in many forms, but good leadership nurtures people out of unhealthy ways of thinking, and not just sweeping the conflict out of sight for a moment.

Understanding the world through the eyes of others can turn enemies into friends.

Your Reputation

Protecting your reputation is not your job. Look at people who feel the need to defend themselves. Efforts to protect their good name does more to harm their reputation than what the slander attempted to destroy. The same is true for you and me. When our reputation is tainted by others, the way we attempt to fix things is usually counterproductive. The person whose goal it is to defend their reputation often does more damage than good. At best, their defensive efforts become a distraction away from the reputation they desire others to see. A hot-headed reaction does more harm than the insult.

Let slander and rumors pass by on their way to the garbage dump. Don't concern yourself with them or touch them. If you get mixed up in it, you will only get the smell of trash on you.

Let me give an example from personal experience. Many years back I was involved in a group where one of the men considered himself to be quite a theologian, and took great pleasure in disproving others. To avoid identifying a person, we'll call him Fred. He insulted anyone who made a comment or added to the discussion. At times, he even belittled those who agreed with him. Looking back I now realize he was insecure, and it came out as arrogance and the need to be the center of attention.

Fred constantly targeted me, and I made the mistake of rebutting his accusations. He would say something like, "You just think," and then would broadcast what he assumed I was thinking. Nearly every time I encountered Fred, he would toss in an accusation of my ill intent or my intent to deceive. His evidence was either a twisting of what I said, or something I never said. I took the bait and would try to disprove his accusations.

One day someone came to me and said, "Why are you and Fred at each other's throats. For a Christian discussion group, you guys aren't acting very Christian-like."

This caught me off guard since I never accused Fred of anything, and all I did was rebut his accusations. Even so, the public perception was that this was a two-way war.

I felt the need to defend my reputation by rebutting each accusation, but in reality I was climbing into the dumpster with the rumor.

Fred gave me a great life lesson in dealing with conflict. There was no way to win Fred over, thus only leaving two other options. Meet aggression with self-defense, or stay focused on the message I was trying to get across. Someone can use rumors and accusations to harm your reputation in the short-term, but your character will prove your reputation in the long run. Once I quit addressing Fred's accusations, people quit saying, "You two keep arguing."

It's a fact of life, there will always be people who will threaten your sense of self-worth. At various times in life you will encounter people whose purpose is to build their ego by taking you and others down. In the end, people will remember you based on what you gave them and not what critics have said. Those who live by the rumor cooler are not your concern. If your sense of self-worth is dependent upon what you believe others think about you, life's mission has already been lost.

Every boss has employees who will speak ill of them – regardless of how much the manager cares and works for their best interest. Every parent will have times when children accuse them of being mean, ignorant, or self-serving. Every married person will have their spouse accuse them of ill will. Every minister will have critics and accusers. These are distractions from your mission in life. Let's learn from the example of Jesus in **John 8:48-51**

> [48] Then the Jews answered and said to Him, "Do we not say rightly that You are a Samaritan and have a demon?"
> [49] Jesus answered, "I do not have a demon; but I honor My Father, and you dishonor Me.
> [50] "And I do not seek My *own* glory; there is One who seeks and judges.
> [51] "Most assuredly, I say to you, if anyone keeps My word he shall never see death."

To be called a Samaritan was the highest insult in that culture. The Jews prided themselves on being pure-blooded and distanced themselves from any Jew who married or were born through any mixed race. To refer to a Jew as a Samaritan served no other purpose than to start a heated brawl.

Notice that Jesus didn't even acknowledge the racial slur thrown at Him. He explained that the message did not come from a demon within Him, but was the revelation of God. To dishonor Jesus because of the message was to dishonor God who sent Him to proclaim that message. He made one statement to clarify the true source of the problem, and then He put all the focus back on His message of life.

What would have happened if Jesus had argued over his pure-blooded heritage? What would have happened if He had allowed the accusation of being demon-possessed to derail Him from the mission? Not one time does Jesus revisit the assault on His reputation. If you continue reading this passage, you'll see His accusers again reiterate that He was possessed. Since the only argument He acknowledged was the accusation that He was demonic, they attempted to distract Him with this argument. Jesus didn't take the bait. He stayed focused on His message of life.

His enemies could never be persuaded, but that wasn't His concern. The message wasn't for His enemies, but for those who were responding. In the midst of hostile critics, Jesus was still able to get the message out and people responded.

What happened to the message of those slandering Jesus? Does it stand today? Whose message prevailed? We don't even know who these men were, but the message of life still goes out today.

The same is true for you. Hostility against you as a person is not your concern. What do you believe? What are you trying to accomplish? What are you leading people to discover?

If you don't have a purpose, you can't lead others to that purpose. Someone who doesn't know where they are going will be easily distracted by critics. Someone who has a purpose behind their leadership must find ways to communicate that purpose in clear and simple terms, and not be derailed by criticism or slander. Your purpose may be as simple as teaching your kids why faith is the foundation of life, or as complex as turning around a failing company. Critics are a part of life. Anyone accomplishing anything will have critics.

Staying focused on the mission does not mean we become deaf to reasonable criticism, but that we refuse to lose sight of the mission of life and fall into the pigsty of self-defense. There is an old country saying, "Don't wrestle with a pig in the mud. You'll both get filthy, and the pig likes it."

Abraham Lincoln is a great example of leadership. Lincoln did not have a type-A personality. He was soft-spoken and didn't dominate others. When Lincoln won the presidency, he picked a cabinet of type-A personalities. Even when he picked out his Secretary of War, he picked Edwin Stanton, his enemy and biggest critic. When asked why he would do such a thing, Abe said, "If he attacks me this way, what will he do to our enemies?"

Lincoln's cabinet members jockeyed for dominance. Most believed they could overrun the soft spoken president. In the first cabinet meeting he presented a problem to be resolved. Each one gave their argument and pressured him to give them control. For the majority of the meeting he sat and listened to everyone's power struggle and solutions. He then stood up, thanked them for their input and said, "Okay men, this is what we are going to do."

What a great example of leadership. This proves that someone doesn't have to have a dominant personality to be a leader. Nor do we have to fear those who believe they can manipulate or subdue us with criticism or demands. It also shows how we can glean from advice, even harsh advice, without losing sight of our mission.

Lincoln also found another way of encouraging himself. During his presidency, the nation was divided and any decision made would be met with harsh criticism from one side or the other – or both. Newspapers mocked his leadership, appearance, heritage, called him evil, and critics used any method possible to hurt him. One day he received a letter of encouragement. It meant so much to him that he kept it with him until the day he died. At

Lincoln's death, the one-page letter was in his pocket.

When he needed encouragement, he didn't let the words of critics drag him down. He reminded himself that there were people out there who saw the value in his mission. He wasn't serving for his critics. He was bringing about change that was good, and he reminded himself of the value of that mission with a single letter of encouragement. It may have been one letter, but how many people stood behind that letter?

Now let me ask you a question. How many people do you think can name a single person that stood against Lincoln? If not for his assassination, few could even name one – and that one accomplished nothing. He didn't accomplish anything of his own merits, and he couldn't stop the changing tide of transforming America from slavery of some to freedom for all.

Unless your goal is to be re-elected, leadership is not a popularity contest. Those who make it so accomplish little. A politician whose goal it is to stay in office only stands on issues that will keep him or her in good will with the masses. A self-serving goal doesn't change lives or accomplish much of value. Leadership is to do what is right regardless of where the mob is going or what the mob believes. A mob can be incited for a time, but true leadership empowers long-term results.

One of the critical lessons of leadership that will benefit you greatly is to forget about your reputation. Character is who you are based on what you believe. A person who stands upon their character cannot lose their reputation. Certainly there will be people of little character who base their opinions on rumor and gossip. They are not your concern.

Even if slander appears to derail your mission for the moment, it cannot derail your God ordained mission completely. It can only alter where, how, or when that mission comes to fruition. Only abandoning your call can take you out of your purpose.

It is not your responsibility to defend your reputation or good name. Your character cannot be destroyed by words – only by your own actions. Your reputation is not saved by defending it. It is reinforced by you becoming a person of integrity. A rumor cannot stand in the presence of someone who refuses to be distracted from their mission in life.

It is not your purpose to change anyone. Not your kids, spouse, coworkers, or any other person. Your lifestyle of leadership will impact others. Once someone observes stability in your life, it will affect them. Some will try to knock you down. This is not your problem. Some will want to know what you have that they don't. This is your opportunity to invest your life into theirs – whether that be on a large or small scale.

Know where you're going and what you desire to invest into others. Then don't worry about anyone not going where you are going. A leader is someone who is going somewhere. Lead in that direction and let anyone who will join you in that calling.

Establishing Your Identity

As stated before, your leadership will not be as effective until you are established and secure in your identity. Your identity will be flawed as long as your sense of self-worth is drawing from your fragile ego. Every person has an ego, and anyone who draws their sense of self-esteem from what their ego feeds them is walking on thin glass.

Someone whose sense of self-worth is based on the circular dependence of emotions, ego, and self-esteem is destined for frustration. The ego is fragile, so anyone dependent upon the affirmation of emotions or circumstances will feel the need to defend their identity. The first self-centered weapon to be deployed is usually an emotional reaction.

If my sense of self-worth is dependent upon itself, I can do nothing other than get defensive when self is threatened. Criticism is painful when I am dependent upon ego for self-worth. Then my only sense of affirmation is short-term success and the affirmation of others. When that need isn't being met, I have to build it up by finding ways to make others notice.

People cry out, "Look at me," through varying methods. Sometimes this is bragging or arrogance. For others it's over-working as they attempt to gain measurable success. For some, it comes out as anger and frustration. Still others express it in self-destructive behaviors or an emotional collapse.

Every personality has its own way of trying to fulfill the need for affirmation.

Each person has these basic needs: to feel valued, to find significance, and experience love. Your ego is a lousy source for these things, and it's unfair to demand your own ego to meet this need. Equally unfair is to put this burden upon others, for no person can fully satisfy your need of fulfillment. If you can't fulfill your own needs, how can you be expected to meet this need in another person? And how can you expect them to meet this need in you?

When your friends, family, and co-workers fail you, it's easy to become bitter, but here's a secret. You fail them, too. We only see from a self-centered point of view, but our quest for fulfillment cannot be fulfilled by others. Their sense of fulfillment cannot be met by you. Flawed human nature can never become a sure foundation that gives us value, significance, and love.

On the other hand, there is no greater person of confidence than the person who understands their identity in Christ. The church frequently adopts the culture's performance based view of acceptance, but you aren't called to perform for God. God is not interested in what you can do for him. God calls for one thing – rest your confidence fully in the love and acceptance He has given you through Christ. Until this is a reality in your life, lasting peace and security will always be just out of reach.

Let's look at a few verses that will help establish you in a confident relationship with God. First look at **1 Peter 2:5**

> You also, as living stones, are being built up a spiritual house, a holy priesthood, to offer up spiritual sacrifices acceptable to God through Jesus Christ.

Let's tie this into Jesus' own words in **Luke 4:18-20**

> [18] "The Spirit of the LORD *is* upon Me, Because He has anointed Me To preach the gospel to *the* poor; He has sent Me to heal the brokenhearted, To proclaim liberty to *the* captives And recovery of sight to *the* blind, To set at liberty those who are oppressed;
> [19] To proclaim the acceptable year of the LORD."

You are not trying to find acceptance with God. True confidence is born out of a heart that is established in the truth that you are already accepted by God through Christ.

No one stands on their own merits. You are completely accepted by God through Christ. The person who trusts in Christ is completely accepted by God apart from their accomplishments or performance. Those who understand this find true self-worth, and their self-confidence is established in the fact that God favors them, instead of trying to build confidence on the shifting sand of praise, affirmation, or what others feel about them at the moment.

When you are confident in who you are in Christ, you will be confident in who you are in this life. Once your sense of self-worth is not based on performance, you are free from that form of self-bondage and are free from the need to defend your ego. There is no longer anything to defend, for the only one who matters is the Lord, and He has already said you are accepted. There is nothing you can do that will make you more or less acceptable, for you stand on what Christ accomplished for you – and your mistakes and successes cannot add to or take away from that perfect work.

Understanding the complete acceptance of God will do more to establish your confidence than anything else in life. Let me add another word of this promise from

1 John 4:16-19

> [16] And we have known and believed the love that God has for us. God is love, and he who abides in love abides in God, and God in him.
> [17] Love has been perfected among us in this: that we may have boldness in the day of judgment; because as He is, so are we in this world.
> [18] There is no fear in love; but perfect love casts out fear, because fear involves torment. But he who fears has not been made perfect in love.
> [19] We love Him because He first loved us.

Notice where we find the true source of confidence, "We have known and believed the love God has for us." When you trust in the truth that God is love, and grace is the expression of God's love toward you, true confidence will emerge. The love of God is based on this one truth – God is love. God doesn't love you because you measured up to a good enough standard. God loves you because that is who He is. Since God is love, He loves you because of Himself and not because of your performance.

This means that when your performance fails, His love does not. The person with a flawed view of love will forever be trying to measure up to the standard of God, not realizing this is an impossible standard. Not only that, they are trying to achieve an acceptance that has already been given. Let me share one last verse on this topic. Look at **Ephesians 1:6**

> To the praise of the glory of His grace, by which He has made us accepted in the Beloved.

This section of the Bible begins by teaching that God chose us in Christ according to the good pleasure of His own will. Because it was God's will to do so, He made you accepted in the Beloved (Christ). You are in Christ because you trusted in His work, and you are acceptable to God because you are in Christ.

This is your identity. God so loved you that He gave Himself through Christ, took away your sins and everything unacceptable to God through His cross, and now you are acceptable to God because of Christ. By acceptable, this means you are completely accepted. God is not looking for leaders who will measure up. God is looking for leaders who trust in Him and are willing to be established on the merits of Christ's good works.

The Bible says that without faith it is impossible to please God. The one who trusts Him, believes in the love God has for them, and looks expectantly to Christ as their rock, is the one who is established on a solid foundation. From this foundation everything flows. There is no fear, for we now understand that we are perfected through the work of God's love. We don't fear judgment, for we stand on the merits of Christ. We don't fear failure, for God promises to lead us down the path He has prepared beforehand, and then open doors that no one can shut. We don't fear criticism, for our self-worth is now founded upon Christ and is not dependent upon our ego.

The Christian leader, if he or she is grounded in confidence in Christ, is more equipped to lead than anyone else. There have been many examples of bad Christian leadership throughout history. Most of us have witnessed leadership that is dependent upon ego, however, bad Christian leadership doesn't change these basic truths. The heart established on the firm foundation of God's

Establishing Your Identity

acceptance can lead effectively – even when navigating through the waters of failure, personal sacrifice, and criticism.

When a Christian leader makes mistakes, instead of defeat, these become tools to lead us into a deeper trust in Christ. God is not limited by your failure. God is not dependent upon your success. You are dependent upon Him, and He is able to transform failure into success and use under-equipped leaders to accomplish whatever He desires.

If your identity is based on your talents, successes, personality, or anything of yourself, you are cutting yourself short. If your identity is founded in the love of God established for you in Christ, nothing can shake you from that firm foundation. Confidence is the natural result of faith in Him. Trust in His love. Trust in His strength. You are favored, and herein lies your source of unshakeable confidence. Anything else is built upon sand.

The Power of Positive Assumptions

As stated several times previously, perception is reality to each person. The person with a negative perception will have negative experiences. Someone who has a positive outlook will usually find good and discover positive results.

Anyone who has served as a manager has probably seen the reality of this truth. Two people facing the same situation will have very different experiences. The person saying, "Why does this always happen to me?" will struggle more than the person who says, "Let's get this done so we can move ahead."

The person complaining will still have to deal with life's problems, but their sour attitude will compound the problem. Each unwanted task will be painful. The problem often takes longer to resolve because motivation is lacking. Solutions will be hard to see because the person is focusing on each dislike and cultivating a negative perception of the problem.

Opportunities often come to those who have positive approaches to life, not because their positive thinking has power in itself, but because their positive attitude is looking for good. Each person finds what they are looking for in problems and situations of life. Good is found in almost every situation, but the negative person is blinded to everything but their problems and methods that can help them escape facing a problem.

The more a negative person focuses on what is negative, the more bad things they will find. A grumbler only sees what he or she dislikes. Someone focused on looking for bad will find what they are looking for. Cooperation is lost because negativism does not produce teamwork. If someone is negative enough, others would rather do all the work than to bear the burden of the complainer. Complaining can't develop healthy relationships. At best, other non-productive complainers may be drawn to feelings of mutual misery, but a group of disenchanted people rarely become productive. However, they often become destructive and undermine the goals they should be working to achieve.

A positive outlook has an opposite outcome. This person faces the same problems, but looks beyond the problem to the solution. A problem stands between them and the comfort they also desire, but they find solutions because they are looking for good. Both the negative and positive outlook finds what they are looking for.

Leadership will always fall short of perfection, for imperfect people are trying to accomplish good things. As a manager, when someone complains about the company, the group, the failures of the job, leadership, and other people, my goal is not to address their complaints, but to cultivate a better attitude. However, when someone approaches with a problem and says, "I have an idea," I know they are not focused on what is wrong, but looking for a good way to resolve the problem. They aren't focused on failure, but are looking beyond failure to the good they believe can be attained.

Don't tell others what you don't like. Tell them your vision for making it better. We have the perfect example in Christ. Look at **Hebrews 12:1-3**

> ¹ Therefore we also, since we are surrounded by so great a cloud of witnesses, let us lay aside every weight, and the sin which so easily ensnares *us*, and let us run with endurance the race that is set before us,
> ² looking unto Jesus, the author and finisher of *our* faith, who for the joy that was set before Him endured the cross, despising the shame, and has sat down at the right hand of the throne of God.
> ³ For consider Him who endured such hostility from sinners against Himself, lest you become weary and discouraged in your souls.

Let me draw your attention to a few points that apply to your leadership and life. Jesus despised the cross. It was the place of failure, suffering, shame, and sin. The sin of the world was about to be laid upon Him, and everything wrong in life was represented in the cross.

How did Jesus endure? By focusing on what He despised? By grumbling and complaining? No, Jesus focused on what lay beyond the cross. He wasn't focused on what was wrong with the world, but on the good He was about to bring through the wrongs. He was about to reach through the shame of the cross and pull through it a victory that would benefit any who would receive it.

He was encouraged by the good behind the cross and not the bad standing before Him. He didn't focus on what He despised, but on what He valued.

Now we are called to look to Him and find encouragement in His example. It's only human nature to become discouraged in our souls. All we must do is look at what's wrong in the world, and discouragement is the natural result. Yet as Christians we have been given the power to have the mind of Christ. Let this mind be in you, lest you become discouraged in your souls.

We live in a fallen world. There are things wrong and people are flawed. Anyone can toss their hands up and say, "What's the use?" Anyone can grumble their way through life. We have the option to say, "This is stupid," and make the unfair or unreasonable requirements into a drudgery. Or we can determine to look beyond what is wrong and find good to pull out from behind what we despise. We can look beyond what we dislike to the good before us, and lay hold of the good that is within our grasp.

As a new manager, an employee came to me almost daily with his complaints about the company. He would let the frustrations of life get under his skin until he felt exacerbated. I wasn't his direct manager, but he came to me because I was the only one who would let him vent. After he went down his list of complaints, I'd say, "Antonio, when they make us CEO for a day, we'll fix everything." He'd laugh and go back to build up a new set of frustrations.

Neither of our phones ever rang, so we had to settle on letting the company CEO run things his way. We were able to make many positive changes throughout the years, but not one of these changes came through venting about the company and the world. Not one solution came through these complaining sessions. My only goal was to get him to release his tension so he could work and not frustrate those around him. All of our solutions came through planning sessions where people identified a breakdown and looked for a way to improve a process. Or remove a counterproductive process.

Why is team building so effective? Have you noticed that the most innovative companies are also known for creating a fun atmosphere? As companies grow, many push the unnecessary cost of employee benefits out of the way to save on expenses, but it also begins to change the attitudes of employees. Obviously, there must be a balance, but the more positive employees are, the more productive, creative, and solution-minded they become.

Power of Positive Assumptions

When your assumption is that a solution can be found, you will become solution minded. When your assumption is that a company cares, you will become more productive. When your assumption is that a company welcomes creativity, the more creative you will become in finding methods, ideas, and improvements. This is true in corporations, churches, families, and other organizations.

A leader must cultivate this positive assumption in others. Otherwise, people tend to gravitate toward the negative. A wandering mind will tend to focus on the negative unless the person is intentional about setting their mind on good. It's a leader's responsibility to bring out the best in others, and this starts with bringing out a good attitude. Everyone can learn to be positive, but some patterns of thinking have to be deprogrammed and reprogrammed in better ways. It begins with ourselves, and then we'll be equipped to equip others.

Assuming the Positive in Others

Perception is reality – even if it isn't reality.

This section is for you, the leader. One of the truths of life is that people, including ourselves, tend to assume the worst instead of the best. If someone doesn't speak to us, we assume they must be mad. If someone quits talking when we come in the room, we assume they are gossiping about us.

A good example of this happened to Jan. It was a couple of days from her birthday, and two of her coworkers were going to surprise her with a cake and a card from the team. Some teammates were in the break room. One of the ladies looked around and didn't see any sign of Jan. She passed around the card for people to sign and they talked about who would pick up the cake, get plates, and planned the other details. Then Jan walked in. Everyone fell silent.

There was an awkward silence for a moment, and then some of the ladies excused themselves from the room. The card-holder walked out trying to keep the card inconspicuous, but her demeanor was anything but that.

Jan was hurt. The next time she happened in to a planning session, some of the others stopped their whispering. As most of us tend to do, Jan assumed they were whispering about her with some type of gossip. All types of scenarios ran through her mind, and she began to identify ring leaders. When she'd had enough, she blew up at a teammate and lashed out with angry words. All she knew is that people were avoiding her and acting secretive, then human nature took over from there.

The plan to surprise her with a happy birthday celebration was derailed when Jan assumed the worst. Then the worst became reality in her mind.

I'm not sure why we have this tendency, but we naturally fill in the blanks with an assumption for the worst. It is not only the Jans of the world, but also the Toms who do this as well. It's not only whispers, but even silence can create this reaction. If I am in a negative state of mind and my spouse is silent, it's far too easy to project my negative feelings onto my spouse. If she fills in the gaps of communication with negative assumptions, she will project that onto me in her mind. Then conflict is born and neither side understands why.

The same holds true in organizational leadership. If I assume those above me have ill will, I'll respond with negative feelings as if this were a reality. If I assume those below me don't value my leadership, I'll respond with negative leadership. Even if one person speaks critically of me, that shouldn't cause me to view everyone under the umbrella of my negative feelings toward that comment.

What's more, criticism comes with the territory. A leader cannot please everyone. To appease the masses is to do nothing. People don't like change, so to improve upon a process or take people into a new direction will draw criticism. This is why our focus must be on where we are going and not where we are. Our focus must be on the good and not the obstacles between us and that goal.

To dismantle one process to build a better one always appears to be chaos in the short-term. When construction is underway, it's always messy, inconvenient, and a disruption to people's sense of what is right until it's complete. Any time we change our course of action, we should expect criticism. Anytime we stop doing things the way they have always been done, we shouldn't be surprised when we are met with negative reactions.

Our goal is to encourage others to buy into the change as we stick to the purpose we have put our focus upon. Then trust your decision. Even if an attempt to improve fails, it's still better than doing nothing and wondering why we keep doing things the wrong way.

On the flip-side, though we should anticipate criticism when we show leadership, we should assume good in the will of those around us. Even if someone disagrees with our decision making, we should assume they have good intentions but have limited insight of our goal or the methods necessary to meet that goal. People may not see our vision, but that does not make them enemies. When someone doesn't agree with our goals, they also should not be treated as an enemy.

In daily relationships, our assumption should always be to see good in others. There is power in assuming the best instead of the worst. If you assume the other person is trying to do good, you'll have a good attitude toward that person and this makes for a better relationship. Even if you are wrong and they do harbor ill feelings, what have you lost by assuming the best?

If we assume ill intent in others, we'll read negativity into every situation and comment. If they are out to get us, are we gaining anything by focusing on their negative attitude? If they are not thinking ill and we assume they are, then we have created a breech in our relationship that would not have been present otherwise.

People tend to rise to the expectations of others. If you assume good in the other, and express confidence in their good attitude, people tend to refocus on the positive – even if this wasn't so to begin with. If they don't respond, then the breakdown is not the result of your misunderstanding. Nothing is lost by assuming good. Much can be lost by assuming bad.

The one who assumes the best in others will see the best and be able to cultivate what is positive so it becomes the predominate attribute in that person. The person who looks at work, the challenges of life, and their environment with an eye for good will find good. Then they can bring out the good, focus others onto positive solutions, and will have a clear vision for decision-making.

There is nothing to be lost in assuming positively. A positive person can still respond to what is wrong, but because they are looking for what is right, they won't feel the need to dump all their negative energy into the problem. A negative person makes problems worse because their negative emotions become a greater problem than the problem.

Assume the best in others. Assume their intentions are good unless proven otherwise. Then assume their bad choice is a mistake instead of a threat. Assume there is a positive solution to each problem. Assume your mistakes are life-lessons instead of failures.

You will be amazed at how a positive attitude can improve every situation. Throughout life, you will have to do things that you don't like, and problems are part of every person's life. Since you must endure anyway, why not endure for the joy before you, and find the good God has built into life.

Not one problem has become easier by complaining. Not one burden has become lighter by murmuring. However, many good things have come through a joyful attitude. Not only are problems easier to bear, but a good attitude gleans good from every field of life.

Assume the best and you'll find what you are searching for.

Be Intentional About Leadership

Nothing in this book or in your current knowledge will profit you without a plan for intentional leadership. The world is filled with good advice and inspirational messages, but the majority gets a nod of the head and a passive commitment. We say something like, "I'll have to remember that," but within a few days it falls off our radar screen.

The goal of every leader should be to build leaders. A self-managing person is a leader in their own right. Some will rise to the level of leading others. Others still will outgrow what we have shared and go on to higher achievements. Don't try to hold others back or feel threatened when someone outgrows the nursery.

Doug missed the main purpose of his leadership. Doug loved to disciple leaders. When someone showed signs of leadership, he would invite them into his plan of mentorship. At any given time, Doug had four to six men in his weekly meetings, and he poured his life into these men.

Results varied. A few would drop out of his mentoring program within a few weeks. It wasn't merely a social interaction, but it was a program that required personal effort and time. Some men didn't want to sacrifice TV time, hobbies, or other things. Some didn't like to read. Some had scheduling conflicts. Doug encouraged men to stick with it, but he didn't get discouraged when people dropped out. This is a normal part of the challenge of mentoring.

However, there was one thing that did discourage him. Doug was a pastor of a large church, and he viewed his mentoring as a closed circle. He was great at mentoring, but had a hard time letting people leave his circle.

One day George felt a calling. He had grown much under Doug's mentoring, and when he saw a need in a startup church, he felt led to invest his life in the needs of this church.

Offended at what he viewed as a betrayal, Doug said, "Why are you leaving us. Look at what we have given you."

After a time of discussion, George finally said, "Doug, for the last year you have been emphasizing the importance of going out and doing. Now I see a need, and I feel the call to go out and do. This is an opportunity to put what we have said we believe into practice."

"But there are needs in this church. We have opportunities to go out and do," Doug answered.

"That may be true, but I see many capable leaders here that can step up. I feel the call to take what we've learned and invest it in a church who has said they have a need we can provide."

The conversation ended when Doug saw George's determination to follow his vision to help another organization. Doug conceded the fight, but he never let go of his feelings of betrayal. The relationship ended when George followed his calling.

Did George betray Doug? Absolutely not. Doug's vision was too narrow, and what he didn't understand was that he accomplished something greater than what he had actually planned. George could now go where Doug would never go, and reach people Doug could never reach. The investment of Doug's life into George will now bear fruit beyond what Doug had imagined. He looked at mentorship as the development of his organization, but God was using him to bear fruit beyond his organization.

The truth is that in George, Doug accomplished the highest purpose of his mentorship. When someone outgrows a leader, this is a good thing. In some ways, mentoring is like parenting. When a child matures, conflict arises when the child wants to spread his or her wings, but the parent wants them to stay in the nest.

Effective mentoring takes the relationship beyond the sheep-herding mentality. If someone grows to the point where they know where they are going, and begins reaching for new goals, we should be rejoicing with them and encouraging them to reach for it.

As a manager, I love to see an employee blossom into maturity. I value what they give to my team, and I am sorry to see anyone leave. While my selfish desire mourns the loss, I also rejoice in their success. When someone shares the desire to reach higher, never discourage this. We should be discouraging apathy and questioning when someone reaches for a goal that takes them below their capabilities, but never discourage growth or the launch of a new direction.

When someone accomplishes more than what you have done, rejoice in your opportunity to be a tool in their journey. And don't be discouraged if someone doesn't recognize your role in their life. Both mentoring and parenting are thankless tasks, until someone begins to reflect on their life and sees the foundation you helped lay. Also, we trust in God's promise that if we cast our bread on the waters, after many days it will return to you. Investment into the lives of others rarely produces instant fruit.

An important thing Doug had right was his intentional effort to mentor. He didn't just give a lecture and hoped something would happen. He invited potential leaders into purposeful mentoring. He understood that people would respond in different ways, and some would bear fruit and others would not. Doug invested his life consistently, regardless of the outcome of the individual.

Jesus gave an illustration about spreading the word. Some will fall on good ground. Some will fall on stony ground. Some will fall by the wayside. Those who receive the word on stony ground may indeed rejoice in it, but when the sun beads down on it, the seed is scorched and withers away. This is the person who allows offense to discourage them. Someone who is only short-sighted will not have the endurance to persevere when criticized or when hardship challenges them.

The seed that falls on the wayside is those who receive the word, may even rejoice in it, but the ravens come and snatch it away and it never takes root. People are forgetful hearers. You are a forgetful hearer – and reader. Any good intention will fall by the wayside unless there is an intentional effort to cultivate it. Sometimes we must cultivate it in our own lives. Sometimes we must cultivate it in the lives of others. Casting our words out there will soon be lost unless we follow up with a systematic approach to grow it into maturity.

Some seed will fall among thorns. People whose lives are crowded with other things will never grow into maturity – even if they believe in what you are teaching them. You can encourage them to take out the weeds of life, but you cannot force someone to focus on what you value. If evening sitcoms are more valuable than investing in personal growth, all you can do is ask them to reevaluate what has true importance, but you cannot demand someone to change their values.

We've all been there. I have many hobbies that I enjoy, but many of these had to go to the wayside to make room for what has more value. Hobbies, recreation, and entertainment are good in their proper place, but far too often we sacrifice what has lasting value in order to indulge in what is only good for a moment.

The Bible uses Esau as the example of this. Esau was the firstborn son who would have inherited the greater part of the family's possessions. He came in from a long day hunting and was very hungry. His brother was cooking a pot of stew and refused to give it to Esau. Then Jacob said, "I'll give you a bowl of it IF you will give me your birthright."

Esau said, "What good is my birthright if I starve?" He then sold his long-term benefit for a moment of satisfaction. It's easy to look at Esau and say, "You fool," but our lives are filled with similar decisions. It's far too easy to value what is in front of us – the thing we want and can see – and devalue what will have lasting value in our lives simply because it is a long-term goal. Esau didn't regret his decision until the inheritance and family honors went to his brother. Then he wept with sorrow. He even raged against his brother.

People haven't changed since the ancient biblical times. We see the success of people, the blessings of others, and the maturity they show and wonder, "Why do they get all the breaks? Why are they honored? Why does that person have more understanding?" Then we are tempted with envy and resentment. Rather than envying the success of others, we should be asking what makes their life different?

Success, whatever that may be for your life, isn't for the most talented, most educated, or the one with all of life's breaks. Success is often the fruit of what we have sown. What you sow into your life is what will be reaped in your life. Consider the wise words of **Galatians 6:6-10**

> [6] Let him who is taught the word share in all good things with him who teaches.
>
> [7] Do not be deceived, God is not mocked; for whatever a man sows, that he will also reap.
>
> [8] For he who sows to his flesh will of the flesh reap corruption, but he who sows to the Spirit will of the Spirit reap everlasting life.
>
> [9] And let us not grow weary while doing good, for in due season we shall reap if we do not lose heart.
>
> [10] Therefore, as we have opportunity, let us do good to all, especially to those who are of the household of faith.

There are many lessons to be learned from this passage, and many are outside of the scope of this book. One thing I do want to focus on is the reaping of what you sow in life. If you value entertainment to the point where you invest ten hours or more a week, what do you expect to reap? Perhaps you can win at TV trivia, but is this what you value most?

If you value investing into your life and the life of others, what can you expect to reap? What you sow into your life will come out in your future. What you sow into the lives of others will grow to maturity in them, but this good will also be reaped in your own life.

As Christian leaders, we are not only to invest into other Christians. The promise is to those who do good to all men, and especially when we invest into the lives of those who share our faith. Our investment in others will reap fruit. Sometimes our influence must first reveal to them a need for something greater than short-term enjoyment. The unbeliever may glean a few things, but our investment into those of faith will have a higher yield. The greater benefit is found in the life of those who are applying themselves to faith as they learn from what we are teaching, for they have the ability to understand deeper spiritual truths.

Christian principles can only grow to a certain point in the lives of those who don't have God's Spirit within them. There is no limit to the work of God in the lives of those who walk by faith.

The final example of sowing seeds Jesus gave is the one whose life is good ground. The seed takes root, grows into maturity, and bears much fruit. In Jesus' parable, some will produce thirty-fold, some sixty-fold, and some a hundred-fold. The harvest is always greater than what was sown if a person grows into maturity. Some will do good things. Some we mentor will do great things. Some will do amazing things. Each person grows differently. The only loss is to those who don't grow to maturity. Even so, the loss isn't to us, but to the person who wasted the seed planted into their life.

Mentorship must be intentional. Each leader must find ways to invest their lives into others. This could come in the form of weekly meetings, a mentoring program, accountability to each other, or a lifestyle of fellowship. Each person and each relationship is different. You can mentor someone without making yourself into their mentor. Fellowship over a meal or at a coffee house is the opportunity for you to sow what God has given you into the life of another person.

Plan a way to be intentional about investing your life into others based on your individual situation. A manager may mentor his or her employees. An employee may look for ways to be a positive influence on their manager. A pastor can develop a plan to grow new leaders and future ministers. Peers may meet together for fellowship or Bible study. Prayerfully seek ways to cast your bread onto the waters of the lives of others.

Find ways to be intentional about leadership.
Find ways to keep what you value into focus.
Be intentional about your own personal growth.
Remember that you are favored, and establish yourself so you trust in the love God has for you.
Be the leader you are called to be!

If you enjoyed this book, share it with a friend. Please take a moment to review or rate it on Amazon.

You may enjoy these other books from this author:

- It is Finished! Step out of condemnation and into the completed work of Christ.
- The Victorious Christian Life: Living in Grace and Walking in the Spirit.
- The Promise of a Sound Mind : God's plan for emotional and mental health
- Simple Faith: How every person can experience intimacy with God
- I Called Him Dancer – Christian Fiction
- God Loves the Addict: Experiencing Recovery on the Path of Grace

www.ingramcontent.com/pod-product-compliance
Lightning Source LLC
Chambersburg PA
CBHW071827020426
42331CB00007B/1642